A New True Book

CELLS AND TISSUES

By Leslie Jean LeMaster

This "true book" was prepared under the direction of
William H. Wehrmacher, M.D., FACC, FACP
Clinical Professor of Medicine and
Adjunct Professor of Physiology
Loyola University Stritch School of Medicine
with the help of his granddaughter Cheryl Sabey

CHILDRENS PRESS ®

CHICAGO

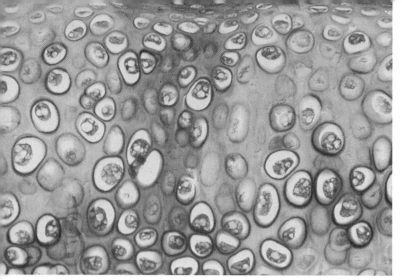

Human bone tissue

PHOTO CREDITS
Journalism Services:
©Harry J. Przekop, Jr.—Cover, 2, 12 (3 photos), 24 (right), 26, 28 (2 photos)
©Bill Smith—31 (bottom right)
©Tom Klute—34 (left)
©Mark Gamba—41

Nawrocki Stock Photo:
©Robert Amft—4 (top)
©Ken Sexton—33 (top)
©J. Steere—42 (top)
©Michael Brohm—42 (bottom)
©Jim Whitmer—43
©Jim Wright—44 (bottom left)

Historical Pictures Service, Chicago—4 (bottom)

Tom Stack & Associates:
©Warren D. Colman—6, 9 (top), 10 (top)
©Dave Davidson—27
©E.J. Cable—24 (left), 34 (right)
©Brian Parker—29
©Terry Kirk—30
©Tom Stack—31 (bottom left)
©Terry Ashley—35 (left)

©Candee Productions—44 (top and bottom right)

Image Finders:
©Bob Skelly—9 (bottom)

EKM-Nepenthe:
©John Maher—10 (bottom right)
©Robert Eckert Jr.—10 (bottom left)

Hillstrom Stock Photo:
©C. Walsh Bellville—15, 22
©Don and Pat Valenti—17
©Tom McCarthy—45

Reinhard Brucker—18

Len Meents—20, 36 (top)

Jerry Hennen—31 (top)

L.V. Bergman & Associates Inc.—35 (right)

Cameramann International—36 (bottom)

Phillis Adler—33 (bottom)

Denoyer-Geppert Co.—39

Cover: Tissue in back of the eye

Library of Congress Cataloging in Publication Data

LeMaster, Leslie Jean.
  Cells and tissues.

  (A New true book)
  Includes index.
  Summary: Describes the nature of the body's cells, protoplasm, tissues, organs, and systems, and explains how they work.
  1. Human biology—Juvenile literature.
[1. Body, Human. 2. Human physiology] I. Title.
QP37.L38 1985   611'.01   85-6695
ISBN 0-516-01266-5   AACR2

TABLE OF CONTENTS

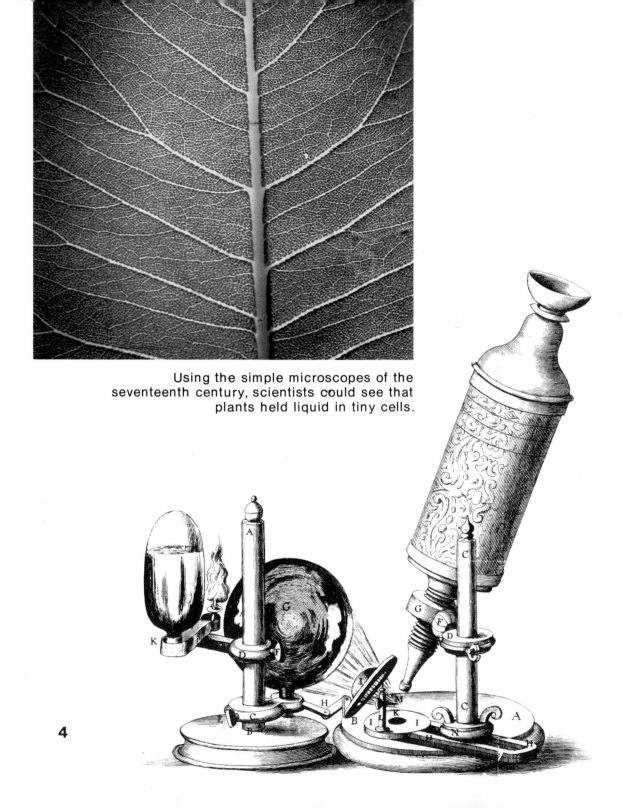

Using the simple microscopes of the seventeenth century, scientists could see that plants held liquid in tiny cells.

4

HISTORY OF THE CELL

For a long time, no one knew what plants and animals were made of. Then, in the seventeenth century, the microscope was invented. Scientists used the microscope to study plants and animals. When sections of living things were magnified under the microscope, tiny structures could be seen for the first time—

structures that the human eye was never able to see before.

In 1665, a scientist named Robert Hooke looked at pieces of cork under his microscope. He saw that the cork was made of very tiny boxes which he called "cells."

Robert Hooke made this drawing of cork as he saw it magnified under his microscope.

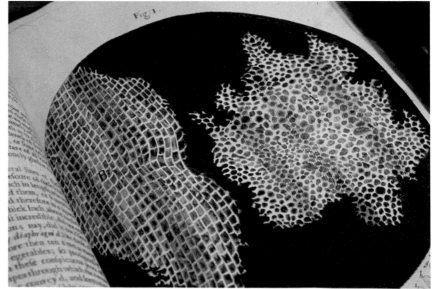

Other scientists believed that if cork were made of tiny cells, other living things might be made of cells, too. By using their microscopes, they found that every living plant and animal they examined was made of cells.

As microscopes were improved, scientists were able to see smaller and smaller organisms. They found that no matter how large or small the

organism was, it was
made of cells.

This led to the cell
theory. According to this
theory, all living things are
made of cells, and all life
activities of each organism
take place in these cells.

Today, very powerful
microscopes are used to
learn even more about the
cell. The cell has proven
to be very complex.

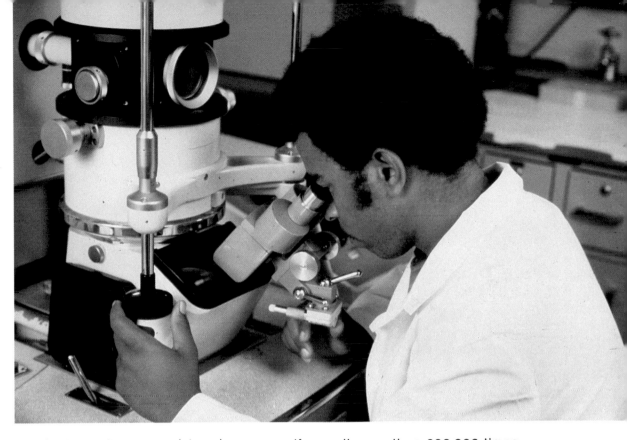

An electron microscope (above) can magnify a cell more than 200,000 times. You can see the nucleus of a magnified plant cell below.

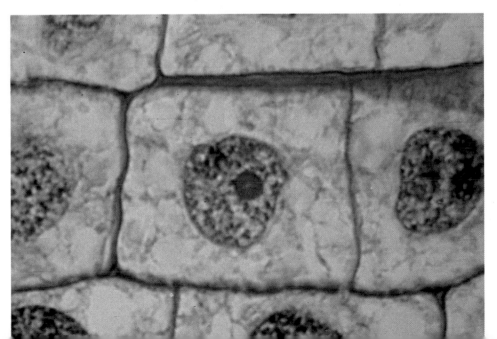

No two people are alike. Each body starts out as one cell. One cell grows into billions of cells that create an individual who looks, thinks, and acts differently than another.

WHAT IS A CELL?

Your body is full of cells. Every part of every living individual is developed from cells. No two individuals are alike.

Most cells are so tiny, they can be seen only under a microscope. Some cells are so small, you could put thousands of them on the period at the end of this sentence.

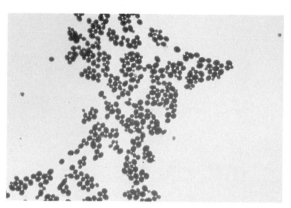

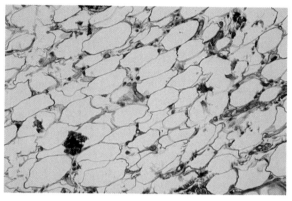

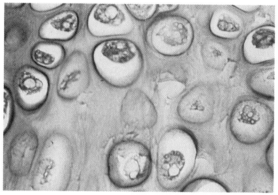

Bacteria cells (above) are among
the smallest of cells. Nerve cells
(top right) can live 100 years.
Bone cells (right) keep the blood
healthy. Magnified 400 times,
you can see the different shapes.

Different kinds of cells
have different shapes.
Some cells are round.
Some are oval. Some are
shaped like spiral rods.
And some are long and
skinny.

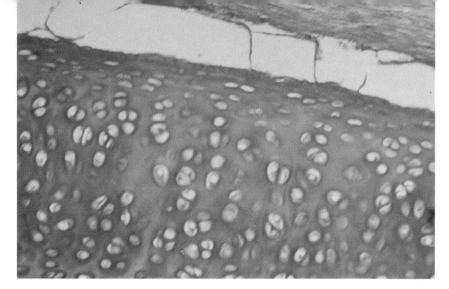

Cells in bone tissue produce blood cells
and release them into the bloodstream.

Certain kinds of cells
group together to form a
tissue. A tissue is a group
of the same kind of cells
that work together to do a
certain job.

Tissues group together
to form an organ. An organ
is made of groups of the

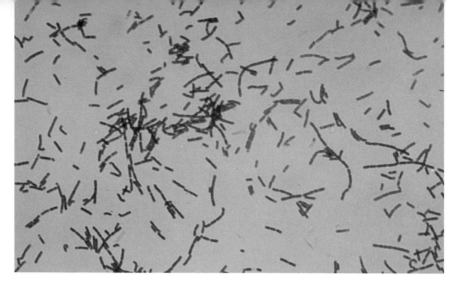
Bacteria cells in chains

same kind of tissues that work together to do a certain job. The different kinds of cells each do a special job.

Some living things, such as bacteria, have only one cell. Larger organisms, like people, are made of billions of cells.

All of the cells in your body came from one single egg cell in your mother's body. When that single cell was fertilized by your father's sperm cell, it began to divide and multiply.

The new cells grew and each split into more new cells. This process continued until every part of your body was formed.

Parents pass on to their children some physical traits, such as eye color and hair color, that they in turn had inherited from their parents. In this way, some characteristics are passed from one generation to the next.

You can think of a cell as the basic unit of life. All cells come from other cells. Life is passed on from one living thing to another by reproduction.

The fibers you see in an orange are cells.

If you cut an orange in half, the fibers that you see are cells. When the orange was cut, the cell walls were broken, and so the juice ran out. You probably didn't even realize that you were dealing with cells!

WHAT IS A CELL MADE OF?

Your cells are covered by a thin membrane, or layer of tissue. This cell membrane holds all the cell material inside it. The membrane also lets food, oxygen, water, and wastes flow in and out of the cell.

Inside each cell is a colorless, jellylike substance called cytoplasm. Cytoplasm

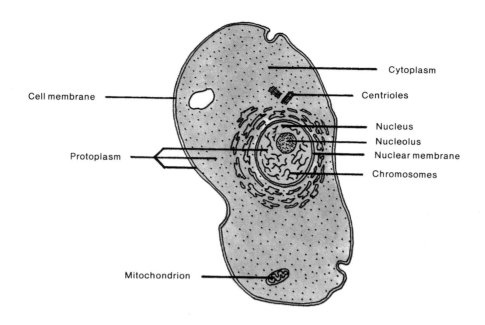

Cytoplasm

Cell membrane

Centrioles

Nucleus
Nucleolus
Nuclear membrane

Protoplasm

Chromosomes

Mitochondrion

contains chemicals that break up food taken into the cell. It produces building materials and energy for the cell to carry on its life activities.

In the middle of the cytoplasm lies a sphere, or ball-shaped structure, surrounded by another membrane. This sphere is called the nucleus. The nucleus controls the cell's activities. It controls how the cell uses food and oxygen. It controls how the cell gets rid of wastes. It controls how the cell reproduces. Without the nucleus, the cell would die.

The nucleus also contains the materials of heredity called chromosomes. Chromosomes determine the sex of an individual.

Chromosomes contain genes that determine the color of the eyes and hair, the physical appearance, and even some talents. Through heredity, chromosomes pass on to an individual some of the traits of the parents.

WHAT IS PROTOPLASM?

The cell membrane, the cytoplasm, and the nucleus make up the protoplasm of the cell. Protoplasm is a chemical substance that regulates all the cell's activities. Protoplasm takes in food and oxygen. It changes food into substances that the cell can use. It gets rid of cell wastes. It repairs the cell and causes the cell to reproduce itself.

WHAT IS A TISSUE?

Cells work together. They are organized into groups. Each group consists of special kinds of cells that do a particular job. Such a group of cells is called a tissue.

Cartilage tissue (below)
Fat tissue (right)

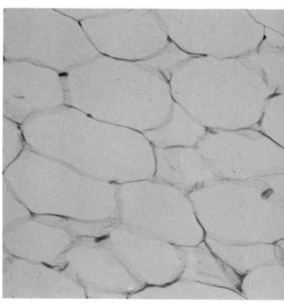

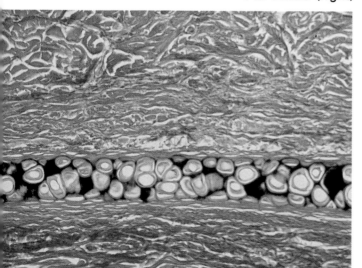

WHAT ARE THE MAIN KINDS OF TISSUES?

Your body contains five main kinds of tissues. For example, tissues that hold muscles together and keep organs in place are called connective tissue. Fat tissue, cartilage, and bone are examples of connective tissue.

Fat makes up about 18 to 28 percent of your body weight. It pads your body,

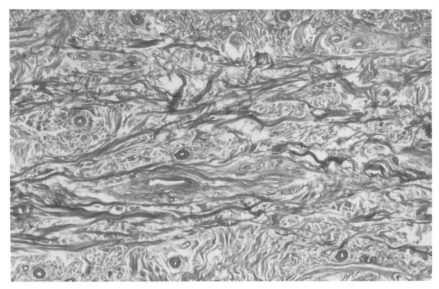

Skin is one type of epithelial tissue. It is made up of sheets of cells that cover and protect the outside of the body.

supplies it with energy, and helps you keep a normal body temperature.

Another kind of tissue is epithelial tissue. The outer layer of skin and the inside lining of the nose, mouth, throat, stomach, and blood vessels are all made of epithelial tissue.

Cells of skeletal muscle tissue are shaped like long fibers.

A third kind of tissue is muscle tissue. It enables the body and parts inside the body to move.

One type of muscle tissue is called skeletal muscle. It is attached to the bones by ligaments and tendons. Another type

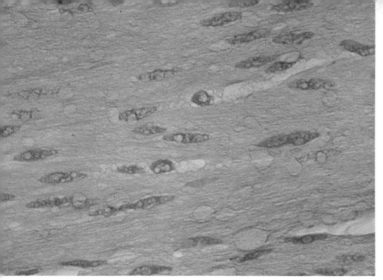

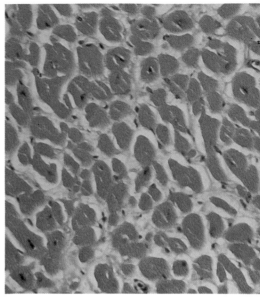

Smooth muscle tissue (above) moves food through the stomach and the intestines. Cardiac muscle tissue (right) moves blood through the heart.

is called smooth muscle. It controls the movement of parts inside the body. Stomach walls are made of smooth muscle tissue. A third kind of muscle tissue is cardiac muscle tissue. It is found in the heart wall.

Human blood magnified 200 times

The fourth kind of tissue
is blood tissue. Blood
tissue is 55 percent liquid
and 45 percent solid. It
supplies cells with food
and oxygen and materials
needed for repair. It

removes wastes from the cells. It also contains cells that fight disease.

The fifth kind of tissue is nerve tissue. Nerve tissue sends messages between the brain and the body to make all parts of the body work together smoothly.

Nerve tissue magnified 50 times

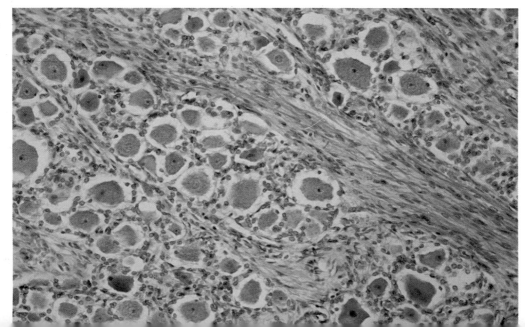

Nerve tissue and muscle tissue work together to make the body move.

WHAT IS AN ORGAN?

Different tissues are organized into groups that work together to do a particular job. These groups of tissues are known as organs.

One example of an organ is the ear. The ear is an organ of hearing. The different parts of the ear are made of certain types of tissue. Each tissue does its particular job. All the

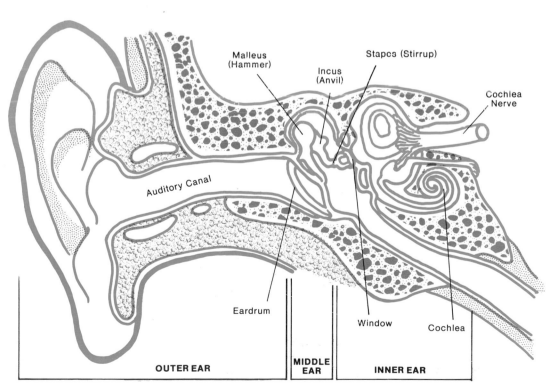

Malleus
(Hammer)

Incus
(Anvil)

Stapes (Stirrup)

Cochlea
Nerve

Auditory Canal

Eardrum

Window

Cochlea

OUTER EAR

MIDDLE EAR

INNER EAR

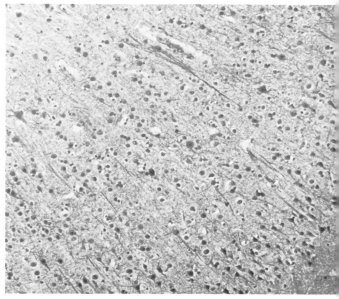

The human brain and spinal cord (left) are complicated organs. More than eight billion cells make up the outer part of the brain. (Below) A close-up of brain tissue

tissues work together so that the ear can perform its job of hearing.

Different examples of organs are the eyes, heart, brain, lungs, and even the

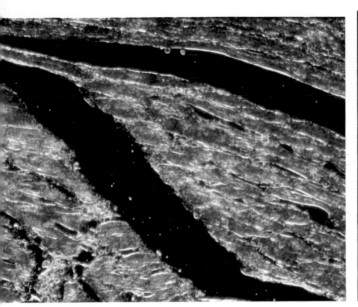
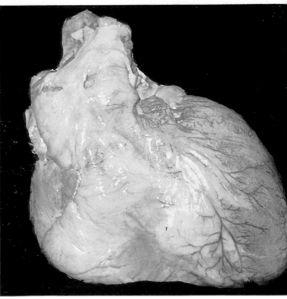

Movement of cardiac muscle (left) enables the heart (above) to beat 70 times a minute.

skin. All the organs have different kinds of tissues that work together so that the organs can work properly.

With all the cells organized in this way, they can efficiently carry on the body's life activities.

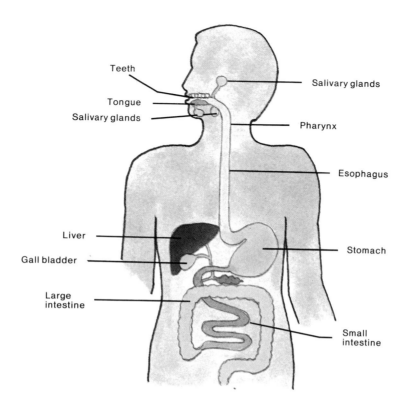

Teeth

Tongue

Salivary glands

Salivary glands

Pharynx

Esophagus

Liver

Gall bladder

Stomach

Large intestine

Small intestine

WHAT IS A SYSTEM?

Organs are organized into systems. Each system of your body does a particular job. Each organ in each system depends on other organs for the body to function properly. For example, to perform the job of digesting food, the digestive system needs the mouth, teeth, tongue, throat, stomach, intestines, and glands.

HOW DO THE SYSTEMS WORK TOGETHER?

Each system in the body depends on other systems to help it do its work. For example, the circulatory system sends blood to all parts of the body. This system relies on the work of the blood, the heart, and the lungs.

The circulatory system depends on the respiratory system to send oxygen

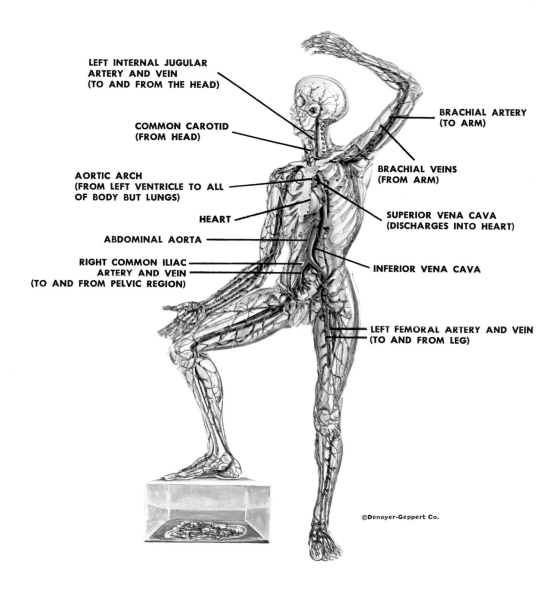

LEFT INTERNAL JUGULAR
ARTERY AND VEIN
(TO AND FROM THE HEAD)

BRACHIAL ARTERY
(TO ARM)

COMMON CAROTID
(FROM HEAD)

BRACHIAL VEINS
(FROM ARM)

AORTIC ARCH
(FROM LEFT VENTRICLE TO ALL
OF BODY BUT LUNGS)

HEART

SUPERIOR VENA CAVA
(DISCHARGES INTO HEART)

ABDOMINAL AORTA

RIGHT COMMON ILIAC
ARTERY AND VEIN
(TO AND FROM PELVIC REGION)

INFERIOR VENA CAVA

LEFT FEMORAL ARTERY AND VEIN
(TO AND FROM LEG)

©Denoyer-Geppert Co.

39

into the blood and to remove waste material such as carbon dioxide.

The circulatory system also depends on the digestive system to break down food so that the blood can carry it to the body cells.

These different systems work together to get food and oxygen to all the cells. The cells are then provided with energy. This energy enables your body's

Cells need food and oxygen in order to work.

system of muscles to do
its job of moving body
parts. It allows the nervous
system to do its job of
sending and receiving
messages.

The human body has more than 10 trillion cells.

Now you can see how
the different systems
depend on each other so
that your body will do all
the things it's supposed to
do!

The cell is the basic unit of life. All cells come from other cells.

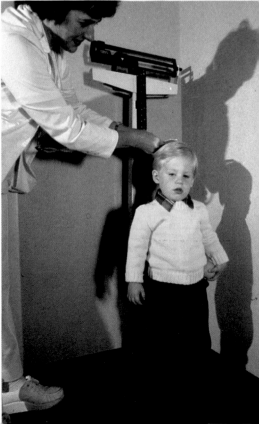

CELLS, CELLS
   THROUGHOUT
ARE WHAT YOUR BODY
   IS ALL ABOUT!
CELLS SO TINY, CELLS
   SO SMALL—
HOW CAN THEY MAKE
   YOUR BODY SO TALL?

WORDS YOU SHOULD KNOW

bacteria (back • TEER • ee • uh) — microscopic plants made of a single cell

blood tissue (BLUHD TISH • u) — the fluid that circulates in the body, carrying food to the cells and removing waste products from them

cell (SELL) — the basic unit of all living things

chromosome (KRO • muh • sewm) — a substance found in cell nuclei that contains materials of heredity

connective tissue (kuh • NEK • tiv TISH • u) — tissue that holds muscles together and holds organs in place, and forms fat, cartilage, and bone

cytoplasm (SITE • uh • plaz • um) — all the material inside cells except the nucleus, that contains chemicals that break up food taken into the cells

epithelial tissue (ep • uh • THEE • lee • ul TISH • u) — tissue that covers and protects parts of the body, including the inside lining of the mouth, throat, stomach, and blood vessels

genes (JEENS) — elements of chromosomes that determine physical appearance, including color of hair and eyes

heredity (huh • RED • ut • ee) — traits passed from a parent to a child through the genes

membrane (MEM • brain) — a thin layer of tissue that covers a cell and holds the cell material inside

muscle tissue (MUSS • ul TISH • u) — tissue that enables body movement

nerve tissue (NURV TISH • u) — tissue that connects the brain and nervous system with parts of the body

nucleus(NOO • klee • us)—a structure in the middle of a cell that controls the cell's activities and holds the cell's hereditary material.

organ(OR • gun)—a group of the same kind of tissues that work together to do a certain job

organism(OR • guh • niz • um)—any living thing

protoplasm(PROHT • uh • plaz • um)—a chemical substance that regulates the activities of a cell

system(SIS • tem)—a group of parts of things that are so related or that act together in such a way that they are considered as a whole, such as the digestive, circulatory, and respiratory systems

tissue(TISH • u)—a group of the same kind of cells that work together to do a certain job

INDEX

About the Author

Leslie Jean LeMaster received a Bachelor of Arts Degree in Psychology and has taken postgraduate courses in Clinical and Physiological Psychology. She has worked in the Child Guidance Clinic at Children's Hospital in northern California, helping parents and children with behavioral problems to interrelate. Other books Ms. LeMaster has written for Childrens Press in the New True Book Series are Your Heart and Blood; Your Brain and Nervous System; Germs; and Bacteria and Viruses. She currently owns and operates her own business in Irvine, California, and is the mother of an eleven-year-old daughter.